FIRST AND ALWAYS

Poems for The Great Ormond Street Children's Hospital

Compiled and edited by
Lawrence Sail
Introduction by Ted Hughes

ff

faber and faber

LONDON · BOSTON

First published in 1988
by Faber and Faber Limited
3 Queen Square London WC1N 3AU

Photoset by Wilmaset Birkenhead Wirral
Printed in Great Britain by
Richard Clay Ltd Bungay Suffolk

This collection © Lawrence Sail, 1988
Foreword © Ted Hughes, 1988

British Library Cataloguing in Publication Data

First and always: poems for Great
Ormond Street Children's Hospital.
1. Poetry in English, 1945– Anthologies
I. Sail, Lawrence 1942– II. Hospital
for Sick Children, London, England
821'.914'08
ISBN 0–571–15374–7

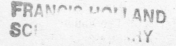

First and Always

Contents

Foreword

Here is an opportunity to buy a book of poems with a good conscience. What you pay for this collection goes whole and intact to the Wishing Well Appeal for Great Ormond Street Children's Hospital. Not a percentage, but the whole sum goes directly to them. Few will disagree, money could hardly be given to a worthier cause, or to one more in need of help.

It was a startling thing to witness, as I did, the chain reaction of acts of goodwill which created, in about thirty days, this anthology.

Lawrence Sail (the editor) became aware of Great Ormond Street's urgent need for funds while his son was a patient there. His impulse to help floated the idea of a collection of new poems, with poets donating their work. The project was taken on by Matthew Evans, Chairman of Faber and Faber, as soon as it was submitted to him. He told Lawrence Sail that the paper suppliers would donate the paper, the printers would donate their labour, the binders would donate theirs, and Faber and Faber would donate all the business of publication.

This unexpected raising of the generosity stakes, from these committees of commerce, galvanized Lawrence Sail, who then spent many hours (one can imagine how many) on the telephone, and writing letters, to communicate this positive, hot surge to some eighty poets. Of these, sixty-three rose to the occasion and produced the poems.

Only two necessary links in the serial circuit of benevolence now needed to be made for the charity, the solidarity, to be complete. The first of these links was that penultimate and by no means least important one, the bookseller. Marvellously this, too, was forged: so that these seven gifts – from the editor, the poets, the paper suppliers, the printers, the binders, the publisher and the bookseller – are now accumulated within the charge of this book. But here they must sit, locked up, until the eighth and final link is made. Which brings us to the buyer.

The simple act that converts all this pent-up energy of goodwill, and completes the circuit, and enables the currency to flow, is, of course, the buyer's payment. Or rather, in this case, what should be called the buyer's gift.

And this is the book's whole purpose: to provide an occasion for you, the buyer, to give the price of it to Great Ormond Street Children's Hospital. The book itself is, in a sense, no more than a guarantee that your donation truly has gone where you aimed it – which, as all givers are aware, is a most satisfying thing to know.

But naturally the editor, and all the contributors, hope that the book will prove to be something more, and that the buyer will find it satisfying in itself – a gift in return.

TED HUGHES

Acknowledgements

The publishers and the editor of the anthology are extremely grateful to the booksellers of Great Britain for their support of this project and to the following printers and suppliers for their cooperation and generosity in producing this book without charge: Wilmaset, Birkenhead, Wirral, for the typesetting; Richard Clay Ltd, Bungay, Suffolk, for the printing and binding; the text was printed on Munken Print NWM 90 gsm supplied by Munkedals AB, through Precision Publishing Papers Ltd; to Aylesbury Studios, Bromley, Kent, for the cover origination; Belmont Press, Northampton, for printing the cover; and WWF Paper Sales UK Ltd, Leatherhead, Surrey, for providing the cover board.

DANNIE ABSE

A Prescription

Sweet-tempered, pestering
young man of Oxford
juggling with ghazals,
tercets, haikus, tankas,
not to mention villanelles,
terzanelles and rondelets;
conversant with the phonetic
kinships of rhyme, assonance
and consonance; the four
nuances of stress, the three
junctions; forget now
the skeletonic couplet,
the heroic couplet, the split
couplet, the poulter's measure;
speak not of englyn
penfyr, englyn milwr;
but westward hasten
to that rising, lonely ground
between the evening rivers,
the alder-gazing rivers,
Mawddach and Dysynni.

Let it be dark when, alone,
you climb the awful mountain
so that you can count the stars.
Ignore the giant shufflings
behind you – put out that torch! –
the far intermittent cries
of the nocturnal birds
  – if birds they are –
their small screams of torture.

[1]

Instead, scholar as you are,
remark the old proverb
how the one who ascends
Cadair Idris at night
comes back in dawn's light
lately mad or a great poet.
Meanwhile, I'll wait here
in this dull room of urine-
flask, weighing-machine,
examination-couch, X-ray screen,
for your return (triumphant
or bizarre) patiently.

FLEUR ADCOCK

Turnip-Heads

Here are the ploughed fields of Middle England;
and here are the scarecrows, flapping polythene arms
over what still, for the moment, looks like England:
bare trees, earth-colours, even a hedge or two.

The scarecrows' coats are fertilizer bags;
their heads (it's hard to see from the swift windows
of the Intercity) are probably 5-litre
containers for some chemical or other.

And what are the scarecrows guarding? Fields of rape?
Plenty of that in Middle England; also
pillage, and certain other medieval
institutions – some things haven't changed,

now that the men of straw are men of plastic.
They wave their rags in fitful semaphore,
in the March wind; our train blurs past them.
Whatever their message was, we seem to have missed it.

GEORGE BARKER

The Mexico Fountains

Hinny my hinny where are those fountains
the Mexico fountains we knew long ago?
Are they gone with the clouds and the flowers of the
    mountains
where the nightshade and the belladonna grow?

Hinny my hinny the midnight is falling
like a flight of dead feathers on those fountains, and on
the summer savannahs the midday is calling
from far to tell us the summer is gone.

Hinny my hinny all the Mexico fountains
are flying and crying through the night and the day.
So hinny come follow the Mexico fountains
Come, hinny my hinny, they are not far away.

PATRICIA BEER

The Scene of the Crime

Today in search of violence
I stand where Carver Doone once stood
Outside the south wall of the church
The only place from which he could
Have taken aim. Where spring had stretched
The graveyard grass he shrank and watched.

There are three windows of clear glass.
He saw her step in from the porch
And bob her white way to the altar
Like someone carrying a torch.
He saw her join the bridegroom, take
Her place, wait for the words to strike.

The pane through which he viewed her then
Faces another, stained with green
And moorland by the hill beyond.
Unclouded in the space between
She was his target and his love.
He raised the gun. She did not move.

The shot made all the crows fly up
As she sank down. The gunman fled.
And I stand where he stood because
I have to live the facts I need.
I must learn something from this spot:
If violence is cold or hot.

Who said that fury lingers on
Where it was felt? The holy stones,
The air, are sending me no message,
Nor is this soil with all its bones.
The tinny chiming of the clock
Tells me that nobody comes back.

Daylight is peeling off the moors.
An avalanche to the deaf, it slips
Down to the stream. Raw evening rusts
My fantasy and skins my lips.
The onset of the dark makes clear
That Carver Doone was never here.

Neither was R.D.Blackmore if
The leaflet in the church is right.
I must go underground to see
If violence is black or white,
Away from here where nothing bad
Occurred, to where it really did.

JAMES BERRY

Hungry-Time Boy Blues

Fo every girl and boy with no-dinner

Yu come home fram school
little less a fool
yu si noh little food.
Yu sey, whas the good!

Table and cupboard empty.
Whole-yard empty.
Fireside dead
and notn said.

Noh little sugar –
me to av ashes-and-water?
Noh one crumb a bun –
me to eat dirt baked in hot-sun?

Boy, this yah time
a real devil time –
a-wahn mek dry bone
outa people and home.

And dohn come by wheel or foot.
Hardtime jus come tek root.
Come and dohn ask.
Never help a single task.

So leaf them rusty.
Place all dusty.
River them dry and gone
with people a-try to go on.

Hear wha me sey noh,
hear wha me sey noh,
spider-leg jackass them goin walk
a-carry skeleton them to work.

EAVAN BOLAND

The Black Lace Fan My Mother Gave Me

It was the first gift he ever gave her,
buying it for five francs in the Galeries
in pre-war Paris. It was stifling.
A starless drought made the nights stormy.

They stayed in the city for the summer.
They met in cafés. She was always early.
He was late. That evening he was later.
They wrapped the fan. He looked at his watch.

She looked down the Boulevard des Capucines.
She ordered more coffee. She stood up.
The streets were emptying. The heat was killing.
She thought the distance smelled of rain and lightning.

These are wild roses, appliquéd on silk
by hand, darkly picked, stitched boldly, quickly.
The rest is tortoiseshell and has the reticent,
clear patience of its element. It is

a worn-out, underwater bullion and it keeps,
even now, an inference of its violation.
The lace is overcast as if the weather
it opened for and offset had entered it.

[7]

The past is an empty café terrace.
An airless dusk before thunder. A man running.
And no way now to know what happened then –
none at all – unless, of course, you improvise:

The blackbird on this first sultry morning,
in summer, finding buds, worms, fruit,
feels the heat. Suddenly she puts out her wing –
the whole, full, flirtatious span of it.

ALAN BROWNJOHN

Heard in a Dream

'We'll direct *Avarice* through a prism
To colour it like *Consumerism*;

And then give *Envy* a cleaner face
As *Competitiveness* – that's no disgrace;

Take *Sloth* from the class where it is the norm,
And give it to the rich as *Tax Reform*;

Move *Lechery* over into the *Sun*
As *Entertainment* for everyone;

Turn ravening *Gluttony* inside out,
There's a *Nose for Business* in every snout;

Tell *Anger* it may shoot to kill
As long as the gun is our *Regime's Will*;

And for a climax, raise private *Pride*
Into phallic warheads, so as to provide
For our country's *Strength* to be glorified.

As for the needy, the old and the lame,
They must learn the rules of a different game,

Where one basic principle applies,
The name of which is *Enterprise*.

If they have more nightmares than sweet dreams,
They can chase them away with private schemes,

They can count up their pennies and do their sums
And save for insurance premiums,

And if the dole and the benefit
Don't cover ten per cent of it,

That's not the job of the Commonweal,
It's for *Charity* to provide and heal.

– You aren't with *BUPA* or *PPP*?
Oh, that's neglect! That's infamy!
You'll have to depend on *Charity*.

Stop whingeing about "the money bags",
And get out there with your tins and flags,

Collect from the claimant-in-the-street
And tell him to stand on his own two feet,

Set up pub raffles and club bazaars
And ten-hour programmes with chat-show stars:

When it comes down to the nitty-gritty,
It's the widows' mites from the inner city

Must pay for their cardiac operations,
The responsibility is *not* the nation's . . .'

*   *   *

As the ranting voice became a scream
I knew I was reaching the end of the dream

Whose words would vanish utterly
Into one giant undersea
Collecting-bin known as *History*.

DAVID CONSTANTINE

Mandeville

He saw the agave flower and knew
A woman who had watched the phoenix burning
But for the once-in-a-lifetime flooding of the Labyrinth
He found no witnesses and yet
It was the story he told best: how when
It happened the creatures congregated
To play in the turbulence as though this were
The bursting well which lies at the heart of Paradise
And swimmers passed, dreaming hand in hand,
Over the corridors of the Labyrinth
And viewed them from a height
Like Icarus. He evoked
The coming up of water
Out of the deep ear: the sob,
The chuckle, water's cleverness,
Her delight in rapidly solving intricacies,

He remembered this. I asked
Where was the Minotaurus when the waters rose?
He answered: the Minotaurus slept
The heavy head succumbed on his folded arms
Like a beaten boy, he wept, he wept,
He dreamed himself a bubbling source of joy.

TONY CURTIS

Sick Child (*after Munch*)

Red-haired Sophie
Pillowed in bed, wrecked
Against the headboard.

Caught in the undertow of a treacherous tide,
Her blood swirls in a wash of the sea.
Tuberculosis has scoured her out like a shell.

At the bedside her mother sits doubled
With the ache of certain loss,
Her face bleared into her chest.

She holds to Sophie, fingers curled so firmly, so long
Around fingers that the knuckles are flushed red
Like rocks poised for the sky's spilling of dawn.

Frail anemone the child against the coral pillow,
Weed-green the bedcover,
Driftwood the table and cupboard.

The mother's tight, black hair is tied and twisted back,
Her body curled and falling in a slow
Black wave over a deep rock.

Airy Hall Ward

There will be days when you or I are bedridden,
Unable to stomach direct light or a voice:
Who fly-posts town?
Word spreads faster than the virus
Rusting the joints; weeks' worth of picked fruit
Turns the whole place into an orchard.

It's enough to make anyone get up,
All this loving and understanding
That's just there for when
You're in a bad way
And all the time I'm thinking
They must have the wrong address altogether:

The door-knocker that had to be silenced
With a bandage, the children shooed
From the sick part of the house –
Partitioned, horticulturally sound,
And a solid stillness
You had to whisper in and labour through.

DONALD DAVIE

Equestrian Sestina

Horse, our poor creature, we treat as if elemental,
Stupidly. This is unfeeling. True, he is fabulous;
Goes, though, not like the wind, whatever his mettle;
Nor, much as he ripples in motion, is he conditioned
By a sky-god's whims, like a river. Not there did the Norman
Culture, that made him its talisman, ground its attachment.

Rather, he was their technology; unsentimental
Reasons made barons and bishops, bloodthirsty and
    emulous,
Curry, caparison into the finest fettle
Him their scout-car, halftrack, their efficient
Weapon-carrier. Dearer to them than Woman
The destrier trampling the Legate's obstructive parchment.

Why then so often, seeking a type for the gentle
And powerful, such as we once were, needing a stimulus
Even to think of that humanness lost, do we settle
On him, on the horse? Why are our horses commissioned
To stand in for what we think best in ourselves, for a yeoman
Sturdiness, or knighthood blurred in a lozengy hatchment?

Is it their having, except for holiday rental
Like jeeps or a sand-yacht, vanished, that now they compel us
Only as fluid, their hoofbeats soft as a petal
Floating to earth on a moonlit hill? A deficient
Sense for the civic has exiled even the Roman
Charger, all laurel and bronze, to eerie detachment.

This has us craning, to trace on a pock-marked lintel
The arms of Sir Hugo, the psychopath. Miscreant, infamous

Cavalier, his horsemanship counts for little
To earn him remission; yet that, no more, was sufficient.
Time, the sad torrent, has washed off his vices, and no man
Builds jetty or pier in that current, or measures its catchment.

There has to be reason why beings not elemental,
Divine nor supernatural, soothe us as fabulous
Creatures moving among us. A horse of mettle
Or merest Dobbin ought to find us conditioned
To a sorry awe. Call it the flower of Norman
Or Saracen chivalry, this was a noble attachment.

PATRIC DICKINSON

Festival Theatre, Cambridge

The curious thing is this:
After seventy one sees
True past that never was,
A kind of setting free.

But it was there enough:
In a theatre I sit hearing
A song beyond mortal bearing
But like diamond or gold,

Soft, hard, shapers of Time
That is or never was:
Artificers of the thought
Of dying, uncluttered, free;
And a conception of me
Dying young, as I am old.

Privet

There, the trees grow wild,
Are not shaped by hedged minds,
But incline seaward with extended arms,
Incline homeward in uncut garments,
Green, white – the colours of rain.
Are pure impulse, airy angels,
Yet womanly in their provocations
And tall perfumed airs.

And once windows are opened
On their summery surveillance,
We say we cannot return to town –
And keep doors open to
Languorous cloudings,
Breathy insinuations.

CAROL ANN DUFFY

The *Darling* Letters

Some keep them in shoeboxes away from the light,
sore memories blinking out as the lid lifts,
their own recklessness written all over them. *My own* . . .
Private jokes, no longer comprehended, pull their
   punchlines,
fall flat in the gaps between endearments. *What
are you wearing?*

         Don't ever change.
They start with *Darling*; end in recriminations,

absence, sense of loss. Even now, the fist's bud flowers
into trembling, the fingers trace each line and see
the future then. *Always* . . . Nobody burns them,
the *Darling* letters, stiff in their cardboard coffins.

Babykins . . . We all had strange names
which make us blush, as though we'd murdered
someone under an alias, long ago. *I'll die
without you. Die.* Once in a while, alone,
we take them out to read again, the heart thudding
like a spade on buried bones.

DOUGLAS DUNN

Sketches

I

When water's edges ripple, where emigrant fowl
Rest among stubble and wiry tussocks,
November's drizzle wets the midnight owl
And the smudged moon reads from its feathery book.

II

I heard of a child born deaf and dumb
Whose patient teachers taught to read and write.
She wrote all day, wishing that sound would come
To add perfection to taste, touch and sight.

III

The boy in the hedgerow
Thought nothing could be worse
Than lying very still and low
In his nettled remorse.
He'd lifted speckled eggs
To his lips, and blown,
Tasting the deaths, their dregs
Yolked on his fingers, down
His chin, his jersey, cheeks.
Little naked necks,
Infancy beaks,
One opened to an empty groan,
Eternity's acoustics.

IV

It feels like love out of the deep, true past.
The moonlight interviews our eyes.
Wearing the moonlight, let us make it last,
Night after night, sunrise by sunrise.

V

Holding these berries was enough to do it
And I was in the church of stories again
Reading the register of local names
Dead far away, and no one could explain
Strange miles of war to me and years of time
Or why the woman in the hat was weeping.

VI

Not leaves, not puffed-up weightless jute, that dry
Sinuous woodland air bagged and forgotten
By whoever. Heavy even to look at . . .
I didn't dare to put my hand inside;
Instead, I used my stick, and saw
Acorns, an oak wood in a sack, shovelled,
Picked up or scooped, raked by a forester's
Chipped fingernails, or gathered by
Oak grocers, distributors of groves
From occult homelands, suppliers to
Druidic cults in their scattered chapters.
I weighed it on my body which braked
In a skid of arms. We export water,
So why not autumn, acorns, fallen leaves
Or hieroglyphic daylight's pagan pages
Scribbled on a timber sky,
Visionary, undeciphered languages?
I heard feet on the massed leaves, a scuffed
Approach expert over the leaf-hidden paths.
I ran away from the Squirrel Man.

VII

Our dappled nakedness and who we are
Turn into carnal fiction when the light
Dwindles into a single windowed star.
There is no love like ours tonight.

VIII

In the leaf-folding wind, what claw, what twig
Or what ground-toughened fingernail
Scratches the window-pane? What underdog
Is begging me to save him from the gale?

Misshapen Caliban, come in, come in;
Tell me the secrets of your lost
Reality, your Pictish origin.
White music in the storm is a swan's ghost.

Here is a bowl of milk, your dish of brose.
Our kingdoms fell and they are gone;
Our names were sundered when our foundries froze.
No words are left, other than words on stone.

An ostracized dimension fills my house.
He is a lump of me disguised,
Dead blood, antiquity, a dangerous
Anger, impenitent, unmodernized.

D.J. ENRIGHT

Babies

Babies are best. They give no offence
Except to their proper nappies.
Strictly they instruct young mothers,
Ruling with a rattle of iron.
They are the boss by natural selection.
Mothers' Union? Only when babies please.

One of them, at fourteen months, is famous
For trying keys on every aperture,
Spurning knots in the woodwork as spurious.
Will it grow up to be a master burglar
Or unlock the secrets of the universe?
It does not say. It is one of the secrets.

Babies have little religion, other than
Categorical imperatives and feast days,
And no politics, apart from the arms race,
Chronic inflation and minor uprisings.
They move in mysterious ways. God created them
In his image. Which accounts for many things.

U.A. FANTHORPE

Children Imagining a Hospital

For Kingswood County Primary School

I would like kindness, assurance,
A wide selection of books;
Lots of visitors, and a friend

To come and see me:
A bed by the window so I could look at
All the trees and fields, where I could go for a walk.
I'd like a hospital with popcorn to eat.
A place where I have my own way.

I would like HTV all to myself
And people bringing tea round on trollies;
Plenty of presents and plenty of cards
(I would like presents of food).
Things on the walls, like pictures, and things
That hang from the ceiling;
Long corridors to whizz down in wheelchairs.
Not to be left alone.

ROY FISHER

A Sign Illuminated

In honour of something or other –
King Bertie's crowning; the Charter Centenary;
1938 as a whole – the city

decreed that on several occasions there should emerge
from the Depot on Kyotts Lake Road an Illuminated
Bus. On a published route

it would slowly glide through every
suburb and slum in turn. Crowds
might turn out. So it came

cruising on summer evenings, before
the little boys went to their beds, its lights
plain in the sun from as much as a mile off;

those lights were its headlamps and certain thin
patterns of domestic bulbs
all over the coachwork. What the city had picked

was one of its own
retired double-deckers. They'd sliced off the top,
blacked the windows, painted out the livery;

it was a vehicle so old
that the shadowy driver sat exposed above the engine
in an open cab. Among the little boys

were many who knew the design and the period
registration plates. In the sunset light
they could take it all in: this emblem

that trundled past all the stops; possessed no
route number, passengers or conductor; was less
than a bus, let alone less than lit up.

Prognosis

Data-crazy, we watch for signs
of creeping disease in the body politic,
knowing the cancerous wound, the Right-wing coup,
was once a mere hiccup in the DNA
or a dotty cabal in a beer-hall huddle.

Always fighting the war just won,
the last malarial swamp is drained
while elsewhere a simian virus jumps:
rumour at first, confined beyond the pale,
a mutter on the edge of the sober city,
the tenuous thread becomes a loaded vein,
breaching the culverts of abraded skin.

O we know that health is a will-o'-the-wisp,
always one step beyond our mistimed aim,
as the pole-axed jogger confronts the wall
of terminal infarction. But the myth persists
that somewhere between our hunting fathers
and notional processed prosthetic man
we might still find that median zone
where a safe sun smiles on milk-braced bones
and melanoma is a brand of tiles,
where, through lead-free air to the unstripped trees
on a crisp clear day you can see for miles.

JOHN FULLER

Twelfth Night

The last ten minutes of cake
　　　Stands in its crumbs.
Surviving almonds pose
　　　Like difficult sums.
Soon there'll be nothing left
　　　When a friend comes.

Birds on their clipped feet
　　　No longer play.
Golden fruit is plucked
　　　For the keeping tray.
The star that grazed the ceiling
　　　Is put away.

As, too, the tree itself,
　　　Naked, uncrowned,
Like an old phonograph
　　　Spinning round,
Weeping wax and needles
　　　Though without sound.

This image of our lives
　　　Seems pretty rough,
But what it might be saying is
　　　That all the stuff
That we've already had
　　　Is always enough.

ROY FULLER

Dutch School

The hidden symbolism of the real!
It seems that Dutchmen painted long ago
Ostensibly commonplace interiors,
But in the shadows hands touched guilty things,
And even some lighted gestures sent unease,
Adjacent to burning coals or leper's clappers,
Or partly blocked by red and tuberous fruit.

Procuress, roué, whore – how easily
Such masquerade as mother, father, daughter!
Freudians umpteen years before the letter,
These artists saw that even kitchen scales
Or piano lessons, in the right tint, position,
Will indicate our most profound desires –
For justice, say, or passion that teaches passion.

ROGER GARFITT

Homing In

For Bibiana in Ladywell

Coming to call you for supper,
I enter a visible hush,
the cat's cradle of reflections
your writing-lamp throws on the wall.
No more than glances off whitewash,
three or four spills of light, it seems
to open a luminous depth
of projections and precisions.
One triangle slants its clear field
across another's ridge of light,
as if the stars were focused there,
their constancies, their still waters
crystallized in a quartz of light.

A hand's breadth of transparency,
it forms above your head, one of
the stations I make in passing,
a scallop shell of quiet – and
would vanish if I came closer,
a silence in your own language
that is sounding the dry water
of these stones. I pause in the door,
afraid to break the first hair's breadths
of belonging, threads and sensings
that are making of this spare room
a familiar solitude,
a separateness that is home.

ELIZABETH GARRETT

Wedding Breakfast

A table in the sunlight;
Two cups of black coffee
Against the cloth's impossible white,
And a basket piled with cherries.

How constancy dazzles with its white
Lies! The shadows dark as coffee,
Two cups of tricked light,
A new moon rising on each cherry.

Still life: you can't. Even the light
Is mortal. Death is the bride in white
Tasting first fruits of loss; the slow
Ripening of cherries, blood-bright.

PHILIP GROSS

Petit Mal

Just a flutter
behind your eyes,
a swirl of snow

that melts at my touch
and you wonder why I ask
Where did you go?

What's happening?
'Nothing,' you say.
It's nothing, true:

a tiny death?
A leaving home?
Who knows? Not you.

Not the feverish script
writ by the moving
finger of the EEG.

Not the maze-mandalas,
shadow-maps,
that are all I see

in the brain-scan
negatives. No trace
of the gusts of flight

or free fall
I've felt brush
past me to light

wing-quivering
on your skin, as if
to mark you out. So

slight. So hard
to hold you. Harder still
to let you go.

House of the Deaf

No words. The flickering of hands.
No call up stairwell or across
a hallway. Doors slam as in a silent
film. Each room, each hammer-stroke
stays blanketed in cottonwool.

A radio has numbers, lights.
Bells sway, are soundproof.
Friends disappear behind the shoulder,
gone once they're out of touch. Water's
as quiet as ice. Tin saucepans dropped
kiss the tiled floor like feathers.

Beyond the hedge at times
fire-engines, ambulances glide by,
flash intermittent scarlet, twisting blue.
Lightning above opposing roofs
plays with no consequence of thunder.

The world is clearer, submarine.
Blackbirds in the garden part beaks
like tiny crab-claws glimpsed in a still pool.
Enclosed in some November twilight
a firework's stars give a sudden puff of sand,
golden, dispersing, noiseless.

Carol-singers enter the aquarium.
Their mute lips depict the non-existent
jingle of horses bringing the kings,
the unerring sign language of the sky,
an angel chorus mouthing joy through glass.

SEAMUS HEANEY

The Butter-Print

Who carved on the butter-print's round open face
A cross-hatched head of rye, all jags and bristles?
Why should soft butter bear that sharp device
As if its breast were scored with slivered glass?

When I was small I swallowed an awn of rye.
I felt like a standing crop probed by a scythe.
I took its cut and scare far in and deep
Until, when I coughed and coughed and coughed it up,

My breathing came dawn-cold, so clear and sudden
I might have been inhaling airs from heaven
Where healed and martyred Agatha stares down
At the relic knife as I stared at the awn.

SELIMA HILL

Lilies of the Valley

The flying-helmet my late father wore
smells of seals,
cloud-banks,
German blood.
I stand in silence,
shouldering a broom.
At night I draw huge maps in the mud.
    *

We live in woods,
beside a quivering fire,
tattooing Ban the Bomb signs
on our thighs.
We wrap ourselves in clouds
like sleeping moons.
We'll sing our songs together till we die.
    *

We stay indoors. We dye our jeans and hair.
We sew black lace round everything we wear.
We soak our feet in bowls of turpentine.
Our knickers twinkle like a diamond mine.
    *

Office-workers watch us from their windows
coil like a snake around the square.
NAGASAKI SMELT OF BURNING PIGS. Hush,
he wants to sink his lips into my hair . . .
    *

Tea-coloured soup pervades the Infant school.
The boy I want to sleep with's disappeared.
The one I'm being kissed by looks like Jesus –
his smile, his flowers, his pale ginger beard . . .
    *

As soon as I walk in, my mother knows.
She throws away my banners and my jeans.
I said *I'll march for ever for this garden,
this lily-of-the-valley, this white rose.*
    *

I'm dancing on the air-base with Teresa.
Her father will be furious.
She is blind.
    *

Beneath the planes, beside the muddy river,
we're waiting for the march to move again.
Lost children. Sheena Easton quietly singing.
Three vicars mend a Trident in the rain.

   *

I've got little ones myself,
the airman said,
his uniform as cold and metallic
as lilies-of-the-valley;
panic; tin.

   *

I live on bread the nurses leave in bowls,
while in my dreams the bullets turn to bees:
I feel the sunshine rub against my thighs,
the *drip drip drip* of honey in the trees.

TED HUGHES

Under High Wood

Going up for the assault that morning
They passed the enclosure of prisoners.
'A big German stood at the wire,' he said,
'A big German, and he caught my eye.
And he cursed me. I felt his eye curse me.'

Halfway up the field, the bullet
Hit him in the groin. He rolled
Into a shell-hole. The sun rose and burned.
A sniper clipped his forehead. He wormed
Deeper down. Bullet after bullet
Dug at the crater rim, searching for him.
Another clipped him. Then the sniper stopped.

All that day he lay. He went walks
Along the Heights Road, from Peckett to Midgley,
Down to Mytholmroyd (past Ewood
Of his ancestors, past the high-perched factory
Of his future life). Up the canal bank,
Up Redacre, along and down into Hebden,
Then up into Crimsworth Dene, to their old campground
In the happy valley,
And up over Shackleton Hill, to Widdop,
Back past Greenwood Lea, above Hardcastles,
To Heptonstall –
                                        all day
He walked about that valley, as he lay
Under High Wood in the shell-hole.

I knew the tangle of scar on his temple.

We stood in the young March corn
Of a perfect field. His fortune made.
His life's hope over. Me beside him
Just the age he'd been when that German
Took aim with his eye, and hit him so hard
It brought him and his wife down together,
And his children one after the other.

A misty rain prickled and hazed.
'Here,' he hazarded. 'It was somewhere here.
This is where it happened. I got this far.'

He frowned uphill towards the skyline tree-fringe
As through binoculars
Towards all that was left.

ELIZABETH JENNINGS

Considering Magic

Don't think of magic as a conjuring trick
Or just as fortune-tellers reading hands.
It is a secret which will sometimes break
Through ordinary days, and it depends

Upon right states of mind like good intent,
A love that's kind, a wisdom that is not
Pleased with itself. This sort of magic's meant
To cast a brilliance on dark trains of thought

And guide you through the mazes of the lost,
Lost love, lost people and lost animals.
For this, a sure, deep spell of care is cast

Which never lies and will not play you false.
It banishes the troubles of the past
And is the oldest way of casting spells.

P.J. KAVANAGH

Blackbird in Fulham

A John-the-Baptist bird, it comes before
The light, to pick an aerial
Toothed like a garden rake, put a prong at each shoulder,
Open its beak and be a thurifer
In dark above dank holes between the houses,
Sleek patios and rag- and weed-choked messes.

Too aboriginal to notice these,
Its concentration is on resonance.
Which excavates in sleepers memories
Long overgrown, expensively paved over,
Of innocence unmawkish, love robust.
Its sole belief, that light will come at last.

The point is proved and, casual, it flies elsewhere
To sing more distantly, as though its tune
Was left behind imprinted on the air,
Still legible, though this the second carbon.
And puzzled wakers lie and listen hard
To something moving in the mind's backyard.

GEORGE MACBETH

Homage to Wallace Stevens

The sun was shining, and we ate our chips
Out of two little dunce's-cap-like pokes.

Far out at sea a low-hulled shape was crawling
At mouse-slow speed along the flushed horizon.

I pointed with my zig-zag index finger.

Container ship, I said to Alexander,
Who likes long words, and knows container lorry.

A slow frown furrowed his dark, worried features.

No, no, he murmured, holding up his chip-poke,
No, Daddy George, this a container chip.

And, suddenly, I saw the men in aprons,
The furnace, and the hot fat in the hold there,
A million tons of chipped potatoes frying
In spitting grease upon the sparkling waves.

GEORGE MACKAY BROWN

The Elemental Stone

'I am blessed by stone and the water in the
hollow stone. Light beats about the stone. The
stone has come from the fire at the heart of earth.'

Here, offered, over and over, the stone of
our beginning and end.

The bride: 'I have taken a white rose from
his hand' . . . (And air and fire and snow laboured
and danced also at the forging of root and petal.)

Ploughman and plough unlocked the stone. 'The
stone stands tall in sun and wind and rain, stone
broken into cornstalks, multitudes.'

The fisherman holds a course clear of reef and
crag. 'I will come soon to the well-built stone pier
– wind in the sail – with the bounty of salt and water.'
(The quarry, beyond, is a broken wave of fossils.)

The gravedigger turns his key. Sun and air and
water of grief have fallen briefly on the dead. And
'This stone will be carved with a new good name,' he
says.

And the monk, 'Here we will build arch upon arch,
stone fountains. A candle will burn and shine in a
niche. There will be water of blessing in a worn
eight-sided font. The air between red pillars will
move, night and morning, with the ordered cry of our
mouths.'

CHRISTOPHER MIDDLETON

Take Off

I meant to build a catacomb above you
So the wind will never blow you away

Monday, oiling your elbow, billabong blew
Monday, you drank, sweating like a thunderbolt

I meant a furnace to balloon beneath you
So you will be odd as an ant on a megaphone

Tuesday, dog inspectors, the electorate
Tuesday a snail, ticked with a certificate

I meant to send you foes, whooping for a kill
So I alone, your fancy friend, will hurt you

Wednesday you puff, cool, chatting, a chibook
Wednesday, seven hostages hanged on a hill

I meant this distance to be close to you
It will tango, if you take a look at it

Thursday catapulted melons pelt our town
Thursday, you said, I taste the heaven of time

I bend a sea-horse, hating to straighten him
You pop a pill, cringe, nod at analogy

Friday a fact I gave you, unsteady as rain
Your velvet parasol blotted out the yataghan

No? Did I show you a photograph? Blow on air?
Away you rode, feet on handlebars, whistling

Saturday, humbly, you took all but the pie
Saturday, hot cakes, cognac, kulebiak, potato

Whoever meant you, sylph, to float from a pumpkin
Never to spin is a skill only a banana knows

Sunday, hawkeye, wearing your blue shimoon
Sunday, scream, anger is old, words are unwise

ADRIAN MITCHELL

The One About Fred Astaire

                    No
        it's
            not so much
                    how
        he

            moves so much
                so much
                    as how he
                        stops

        and then moves so
            much again all
                over
                    every
                        anywhere
                        all over
                            so much

        thank you
                Mister Astaire

                    so much

La Jeunesse

Straight from her door
Through rows of vines towards
The river, one white bucket
Swinging for Sunday, the air
Fleshed out with heat
So plump this risen morning
Purpling to ripeness
But not yet, but not quite
Yet among these sunflowers
Leaning their weary faces
Huge and vacant
After her, so stooped
So nodding, and the one
Note tolling distantly
Across the river *mort*
La mort comme ça aussi la mort
From the little church's
Bell-tower on a low hill
Rising from the vines
And ringing, swinging
Its one black upturned
Bucket emptying
All gathered sound this morning
Everywhere *la vie la mort*
Although she has turned already
Walking to her door.

The Revolution

A made world; an artifice; shiny, spooked:
in the right light you could actually see through it.
The right light was rare; well they knew it!
They believed in grin and go; hook, don't get hooked.
Bread and circuses, unbelievable; helicopters, flumes.
Satyagraha? You have only to ask.
Millions were still content to grunt and bask
in designer spas, pink jacaranda rooms
run up a moment before, out of nothing. Power
bursting all round like drunken sonic booms
for those who had ears to hear – earwax took
most of that. We teased their sleazy code, our
drills went in and gouged the viscous looms
they'd programmed. It's the earth, green. Smell! Look!

ANDREW MOTION

Columbia Road

I happened just to be thinking
how twenty-one years ago
a girl I had barely met
lay with me day after day
(lay in my head, I mean)
on a white, deserted beach
or tucked in a crevice of wheat.

And I happened to say her name
aloud in Columbia Road
just as my wife and I
were weaving out one Sunday
past stall after stall of flowers:
Carnations? Chrysanths? Tulips?
Make up your mind. It's murder.

My wife just happened to hear.
Bryony? Did you say Bryony?
I knew a Bryony once –
black eyes; her father farmed.
She died in a car, I think,
and there was a brother, or sister,
or both, or something like that . . .

Then I just happened to see
a square-rigged Victorian ship
sail up to a tiny island
somewhere near the equator,
drop anchor, and put down a boat
which slithered into a bay
of silky, turquoise water

with someone crouched in the prow
who knew from others before him
that here and nowhere else
grew the most beautiful flower
ever to spring in the world,
of a colour made to blind you,
and scent to drive you mad,

and I happened to see him leap
smartly into the shallows

and scale a crumbling cliff
to find the island nothing
but flakes of barren rock
like a white, unpeopled beach,
or a desert of dead grain.

PAUL MULDOON

Poplars

I stepped on a wonky floorboard
and the wardrobe opened of its own accord

to the whinge of curlews
and the garrulous

creaking of frogs.
Among her diaphanous frocks

stood two pairs of muddy
boots. I recognized my own timid

'*Are you going to San Francisco*?'
and his 'I'll show you San Francisco

if you don't button your lip.'
We were holed up

in a gully
between two fields of seedling cauli-

flowers. The barrel of his shotgun
was fusty with catkins

[43]

of willow or alder.
He'd told me once how he'd left Halifax

a week before war was declared
to come home and grow flax

rather than fight as a British soldier.
Was he in some sense a coward?

I made to speak. 'Button your lip.'
A nervous handclap,

then a round of applause
as three wood-pigeons flew out of a blouse

and into the mirror
on the back of the wardrobe door –

its impossibly straight, poplar-flanked
road in northern France.

Enterprise Culture

1159, when John of Salisbury
Writes in his *Metalogicon* about
The followers of Cornificius
(A name derived from Virgil's discommender)
Who 'pay no heed to what philosophy
Teaches, and what it shows that we should seek
Or shun. Their sole ambition', in the words
Of John, 'Is making money: by fair means
If possible, but otherwise by any
Means at all. There's nothing they deem sordid
Or inane except the straits of poverty.
Wisdom's only fruit for them is wealth.'

So much for John of Salisbury – a classic case
Of a moralizing, moaning, so-called thinker.
But now a more hopeful fable for our time:
The case of the loganberry. After great
Creating nature did its bit, along came
Logan to supply the obvious defect:
A red blackberry with an elongated nose.
Everyone's happy: he makes a killing,
And Kate Potosi gets her cut by selling
Them to people who make jam. My point is this:

If John of Salisbury'd taken out a leaf
From Cornificius's book and used his brains
To come up with something practical like that,
He might have saved the whole of western Europe
Centuries of fruitless disputation.

The Hospital for Sick Children

today   today and tomorrow
they'll be melting down
the Artificial Man
– no drums of synthetic whale oil
as Leviathan slurs in the vat
only kids' tears a spent kidney
or a tiny hole in the heart
then the stink of credit cards and BUPA

thirty years back
I waved byebye to my brother
as my mother led him
toward a buffed shiny turbo-prop
on a flat hill above Belfast
– no more rooted
than any stump of petrified wood
in the departure lounge
I could see hares
all windcombed and quivering
in the flixy grass
and radar vans
parked on the perimeter
like military ambulances

she was taking him
to a wooded square
– bookshops hospitals galleries
a dove-grey church a paved street
and all the nurses and doctors
in the whole wide world
would take care of my brother

my hurt sparky brother
whose voice sits in my conscience
as I melt wax for a candle
and strike this one match
in an uncomfortable private place

– fewer and tackier
the hospitals the bookshops the galleries
– fewer the nurses and doctors
but how many Captain Ahabs
go stalking the great broken parks of London
admiring those trees
beached there like whales?

PETER PORTER

Stuff and Chuck

To seek simplicity,
the valency of power,
as when a group of people
bravely disparate
gathers in one room to hear
(I nearly wrote endure)
a Savonarola
lecture them on dust
and lost dubiety,
and feel the warmth of victims
happy to be found some day
like ferns or moths
impacted in their strata:
here is the plot laid out
plainly from the start,

a journey into hunger
and hung with ritual.
It is the stomach
not the mind which now
breaks the magic beam
and opens wide a door
on everlastingness:
to gorge and to be sick
is all that may be done
with images, hoping to find
an empty mystery
which numerals and love
and sore rastrology
might overlook in their
quest for the absolute.

RODNEY PYBUS

And There Was Light

When I was just a wee tourist in the language
my father'd repeat his mother's '*Fiat Lux*!' –
about all he knew of Latin, but it brought her
a mite closer out of the murk that's before-my-time.
(I drop such memories down the well
to hear them bounce and
rattle off the years.)

She caught him once sneaking into the house,
on leave from Flanders where he'd seen bits of his friends
left on trees, and couldn't speak of the horses.
'So it has come to this – ' her voice from the stairs
a tartan of outrage and despair,

black bombazine at full stretch –
'newspapers on the Sabbath!'

'She could have ticked off God,' he said forty years after,
not smiling. I've still the only book she'd touch
on that day when sunlight was forbidden,
curtains pulled against the Devil's glittery sheen.
Her name's there on the fly-leaf, Margaret from Annan
married to James a hundred copperplate years ago
in Cumberland: I know the village –
sandstone the colour of a girl blushing.

Not just the War was skewing her world.
Candles and the slow, sad thrum of gas
had gone: each new-fangled globe
looked more at home in Alma Place
than she ever felt, expecting catastrophe each night
among the Sassenachs of Shields.

Out of sight her family smiled, but
she didn't forget how all our days grow shorter
all the time. She'd go from room to room,
holding her breath till she grew dizzy,
daring it to work, daring it not to work:
click – *'Ah!'* click – *'Ah!'* click – *'Ah yes!'*

PETER REDGROVE

Dark Room

A madonna shaking out scent from her hair.
A lighthouse of scent, shaken out.

There was a red child in the room,
A red child in a photograph.

A second woman sat there
But her hair was grey as moonlight
And coarser
And shook out scent too.

But the younger woman with her dark hair,
That was light and soft
And shook out great beams of perfume.

The illumination: it was a photographer's room,
A red room.

Something was developing in the dark.
She shook the trays.
The child watched peaceably out of them.
Perfume shook out of the chemicals.

She was developing the hundred pictures
In a red room
With the shudder of her hair, that chemistry.

MICHÈLE ROBERTS

The Road to Trento

For Sarah giving birth

White dashes. White dots.
Two white strokes:
a pine tree; a roof.

White pockmarks and scars
on beech trunks. White Vs
on what must be mountains.

Snow, sifted exactly, catches
all horizontals, out-
lines them. White
blocked on to white.

Waves and flurries
of frost
repeat, repeat:
branches fling up and out
like quivering wires.

We force ourselves
gently
through the cold pass

like your child
tobogganing on
your slope
the world turning
itself inside out
the world
turning round

the world
bearing down.

We come down
into the valley
of castles and vineyards
and small white fields
combed with a black comb.

The fruit trees are ice.
I hear your great shout.

CAROL RUMENS

About the Green Oranges

(Leningrad, March 1987)

They sat like a disarmament proposal
On our table in the hotel dining room,
Looking less and less negotiable.
Even the vegetarians flinched from them.

The talks beside the lake weren't going well.
Neither was the turnover in these
Miniature ballistic atrocities
– Which now began to occur at every meal.

Oranges Are Orange. Grass Is Green
– Like policemen's greatcoats. Never Trust A Red.
(It's better to be dead than dyed that shade).
You Can't Tell A *sosiska* By Its Skin . . .

But what about an orange? Feeling less
Hopeful than thirsty on Sadóvaya Street
One day, I bought a mossy half-a-kilo.

The Geneva talks stand just as still, or stiller,
And this is simply a memo, a PS,
To say those green-skinned oranges are sweet.

LAWRENCE SAIL

Rose Garden

For Matthew

Whorl upon whorl, cake-petals
Without charity, pale, brittle,
They flare on their barbed poles.

Brazen as searchlights, they stare
Into the angles, their field of fire
Spreading from the foot of the tower.

Stepping up to them, you sense
How they suck the air, microphones
Themselves blank, without fragrance.

Why do they flourish, where these walls
Lay down the law? Why, still tremble
At boots mashing the gravel?

Orderly, yes – and implying
Dreams of escape. Beyond them, the high
Walls lean in on the sky.

CAROLE SATYAMURTI

Woman in Pink

The big, beautiful, copper-haired
woman in the next bed
is drowning in pink.

She wears pink frilly nightdresses,
pink fluffy cardigan and slippers.
Her 'Get Well' cards carry pink messages.

Her husband brings pink tissues
and a pink china kitten; he pats her head.
She speaks in a pink powder voice.

Yet she is big and beautiful and coppery.
At night she cries bitterly,
coughs and coughs from her broad chest.

I know the cure for her
– I'd take her to the sea, where she'd ride
the deep Atlantic rollers,

split rocks for fossils,
abseil the cliffs
and never wear anything but green.

WILLIAM SCAMMELL

Love & Co

Dinner for two. The candleshine
breeds shadow in a vase of flowers,
inspects the morals of the wine,
the cutlery, the bread, the players,

makes a Rembrandt of a room
that's godless, but for a shining eye.
Bare shoulders sway. The steady flame
picks up the mortice on a key

hanging from the dresser, which
has pockets for as many wares
as grandpa did, its wooden knees
comfortably beneath the stairs.

Truly the world would lock us out
grain by grain and sense by sense.
Love puts its shoulder to the door
with *ad hoc* violence.

A limb here and a limb there
in the double bed, the back of the car.
The candle smothers, nearly; blind
convulsive breathings. Behind

the flower there's always another flower.

Talking Head

Take the unfleshed head, the strict skull;
Hold it in the palm of your left hand
While, with pincers of right forefinger and thumb,
You carefully select a plump, green grape.
Delicately place the grape in the socket
To the left of where the nose once jutted.
If it does not fit perfectly discard it.
Choose another, and another, until you find
One that plugs in snug. Over the twin cavity
Place a black, piratical eye-patch,
Secured by a wide elastic band.
The choice of hat is yours, a beret perhaps,
A tricorne, sou'wester or a large tea-cosy;
Something sporty like a cricket cap or boater;
Nothing, I suggest, explicitly sacerdotal.
Next, into that empty smile, or snarl,
Insert a partly smoked cheroot or half corona.
Then decide on a topic of conversation,
Not too contentious but not tedious either.
Avoid mentioning rivers, bells, masonry and flowers.
Listen carefully and you may be instructed
Though not, I fear, amused or comforted.

MICHAEL SCHMIDT

The Heart Asks

It wasn't snowing but it should have been.
You were an old man, nine months from the grave.
Your hand was very dry and very hot
And large, as I recall (I was a boy,
Fourteen years at most, I led you round
Part of the school, your guide; you seemed to listen).
That night you read in a slow, dismissive voice
That left the words like notes on staves hung in the air,
No longer yours, but part of memory –
You talked about Miss Dickinson of Amherst
And said aloud the eight lines of her poem
'The heart asks pleasure first.' And from that night
I've known the poem word-perfect, part of me.

I think you let more lines free into language
And memory with your rusty, lonely voice
Than any other poet of our age.
It must have been like freeing doves
And watching them go off to neighbouring cotes
Or into the low clouds of your New Hampshire
Knowing they'll meet no harm, that they'll survive
Long after the hand that freed them has decayed.

Those lines are wise in rhythm and they lead
Into a clapboard dwelling, or a field,
Or lives that prey upon the land and one another,
Or the big country where we both were children.

DAVID SCOTT

Bricks

The big difference between us
is that you want to build the house up
and I want to knock the house down.
So you will have to be quick
because as soon as that last brick
is placed on the very, very leaning top,
I'm going to give the whole thing
a tremendous wallop,
and there'll be bricks flying everywhere.
'Don't you dare!'
(Wallop) Brick bombs. Brick rain.
(Long silence)
'Can you build it again?'

E.J. SCOVELL

The Language of Infancy

Empty of knowledge, in your face
Brilliant already consciousness
Lies open like a flower to charm
And draw all in, the swarms of time.

And your wild, moth-blind, tentative
Movements, yet like a homing dove
Straighter than reason understands,
Surer than sight, fly to our hands

And say their word, no word but song.
You press towards language all day long
While yet you cannot sleep nor stir
But what you do sings who you are.

PETER SCUPHAM

Dancing-Shoes

At Time's *Excuse me*, how could you refuse
A Quickstep on his wind-up gramophone?
How long since you wore out your dancing-shoes,

Or his vest-pocket Kodak framed the views
In which you never found yourself alone?
At times, excuse me, how could you refuse

His Roaring Twenties, stepping out in twos,
Love singing in his lightest baritone?
How long since you wore out your dancing-shoes

And shut away that music, hid the clues
By tennis courts long rank and overgrown?
At times, excuse me, how could you refuse

To say his choice was just what you would choose,
Although he spun your fingers to the bone.
How long since you wore out your dancing-shoes?

The Charleston and the Foxtrot and the Blues –
The records end in blur and monotone.
At Time's *Excuse me* – how could you refuse?
How long since you wore out your dancing-shoes?

PENELOPE SHUTTLE

In the Garden

She slip-slops down the path,
her long-legged shadow hunting the slipper.
The greasy stump of the alder
is slippery to my touch,
reeks of cats and their polygamies.
Fuchsias scatter their cache-sexe petals,
crimson and cream, strip-teasing.
I perch and sulk on the wall.
But the girl joins in,
pulling off her jumper
and kneeling, ear to the ground,
listening to what's growing,
what luck's turning.

She loves best (she says)
this one early-summer lily with its twin buds
hoist atop a long step-ladder of chinese-lime leaves,
each bud sweltering out of a swollen purple-streaked
    udder,
and into a milky-blue girlhood,
voluptuous and intact, petals unfisting
as we watch, their perfume a shiver of bodices,
a whiff of aphrodisia;
blue favourites opening up to the sun, glories,
leaving me in the shade, rouged and thoughtful,
my daughter laughing, on hands and knees,
white lace of her difficult blouse puffed up like a solo.

JON SILKIN

Cherokee

On sandstone, barite
makes sand-roses, cabinets of them
in a year of dying. Close, but not close
in kinship, so as to keep those they love
in sight, in the world
next to this, distant
as the odour of plums tossed
in summer wind. The blades of sand-roses
glint, as if touched by mites. They gasp, and smell
of bituminous air. They were
the Cherokees, their forced march
to Oklahoma, their drops of blood
made stone in God's washing tears.

They open, and don't breathe
in the air's
generative lulls. Wherever mercy
is human, don't look
to pity to come like a child
weeping its maternity, perfect
between the hands of the rushing form
of the Shekinah. Creation is
an Indian fury, needs art for its pain,
statues of hurt.

I smell frankincense, pity's herb.
We'd do right
to be scared of it. If I want
another's sacrifice it must be I need
pity manifest. With little faith
I chafe my hands; tenderness

[61]

rubs perfumed between them,
the best, most weeping of grasses,
the least form of life I crop.

C.H. SISSON

Sonnet

If I could speak, then I would speak to you,
And you and you, if I knew who you were,
As I should do, if love could make one sure
Of more than flesh, as it pretends to do:
But flesh alas can lie, as Adam knew,
And as we all know, who have sought the cure
Of our unhappiness in its allure,
Which mirrors our desire, and so is true.
The truth we sought elsewhere is in ourselves,
Yet not there either, for we know by halves
Even our own wishes. How can we know
Others', and still less others who, like us,
Are blind and hopeful, and impervious
To all words not their own, and find us so?

STEPHEN SPENDER

Greek Anthology

To Charles Causley

Above us, is a firmament of stars
Stretching through time five hundred years –
Two thousand more years distant from us.
  Some names still reach us, brilliant as
Jupiter, Orion, Mars –
Anacreon, Meleager, Callimachus.
  Plato still writes across these skies
His longing for their thousand eyes
To gaze down on his friend,star-gazing
– Earth's star – whose eyes must then meet his.
  Some have lines so few they seem
As faint as is their poet's fame.
  I read one who's anonymous.
Out of his world the poet has pressed
One instant of intensest flame
That has burned through the capsule of his name.

GEORGE SZIRTES

Salt

It begins in salt, a pinch of white
added to a mound on a tablecloth
in a friendless boarding-house, where she talks
of striptease and he looks vaguely embarrassed,
makes sucking noises with his mouth,
and hates the elaborately curtained and terraced
six-room establishment with its sixty-watt light
and its proximity to coastal walks.

It begins here, eating out the centre
of the past, an indifferent turning away,
leaving an ache for the vanished
that goes on vanishing, eroding under
wind and sea, an ancient fishlike bay,
a resort that ages badly and turns blander
with each year that heads for winter,
and still the story isn't finished.

Sealed tobacco tins and open drawers
of pale devices, magazines that burn
in hands, the smell of adult beds.
A lit room in a window, the reflection
of a boy writhing like a worm,
the black panes each with its clear section
of interior, of walls and doors
that bear the familiar burdens of his head.

This was the parental home the sea
brought in, its end in its beginning
tail-in-mouth eternally. This cold
and even light that levels out the tones
of summer autumn winter and the spring
within a narrow harmony of bones
and fossils lends domesticity
to secret lives. And now they can be told.

Healing

Sick wards; the sailed beds
becalmed. The nurses tack
hither and fro. The chloroform
breeze rises and falls.
Hospitals are their own
weather; the temperatures
have no relation
to the world outside. The surgeons,
those cunning masters
of navigation, follow
their scalpels' compass through
hurricanes of pain to a calm
harbour. Somewhere far down
in the patient's darkness
where faith died, like a graft
or a transplant, prayer
gets to work, repairing
the soul's tissue, leading
the astonished self between
twin pillars where life's angels
stand wielding their bright swords of flame.

Mother and Child

Big-headed, tidy, about my own age,
He stands attentively beside a woman
I take to be his mother, small and frail.

Then suddenly he blurts some words out, child
Wanting a sweet, clamouring noisily.
Something is wrong with him. I look away.

His mother calms him quietly. He nods
But lets his lower lip tremble, a tear
Roll down his cheek in dumb resentfulness.

How many years they must have lived like this,
Since over half a century ago
She felt the leap of something deep within,

Not knowing what it promised was this child
Who now stands by the counter neatly dressed
In a man's clothes, weeping not like a man.

CHARLES TOMLINSON

Oxen

There are no oxen now in Tuscany.
Once, from any hill-top, you might see
The teams out ploughing, the tilled fields stretch away
Wherever those bowed heads had chamfered round
The swelling contour. The first I ever saw

Strode over ground in such good heart their ease
Was the measure of its tilth. The ploughman knew
His place – behind his beasts, and at the head
Of all the centuries that shaped these hills.
Once, *Belle bestie*, I murmured to myself,
Passing a stall that opened on the road
And catching sight of oxen couched inside.
Belle bestie a voice replied, and I
Was ushered in to touch and to admire
The satin flanks, the presence on the straw.
I recognized the smell, recalled the warmth
Of beasts that rustled all one winter night
In the next room: the stars across Romagna
Pinned out the blackness of the freezing sky
Above a plain that sweat of ox and man
Had brought into fruition. Once I saw
An ox slain in an abattoir. The blood
That flushed the floor was dark and copious –
More than enough to hold the gods at bay
Or bring the dead to speech. The dead spoke then
As every deft stroke of the butcher's men
Revealed an art that was not of a day.
The toughest ground that ever oxen broke
Was by Sant' Antimo. I watched the dust
Turn their slaverings brown and choke the man
Who jolted in their wake and cursed the stones
That cropped out everywhere, unslakeable
The thirst that parched him. He would have been the first
To welcome in the aid that brought his end,
These cheerful tractors turning up the land
Across all Tuscany. No bond of sweat
Cements them to his generations: careless blades
Advancing to the horizon as the clods yield,
Bury both beast and man in one wide field.

CLIVE WILMER

The Garden

Efface complexity, forget the bond
Of old affection, trust, ennui . . . For love,
This room's the world: which all the world beyond,
Although enriched by it, knows nothing of.

Your body is the garden at its heart:
Sweetness and pungency; earth in this place
Is damp, springy with moss, and when I part
The leaves up there, fruit dangles in my face.

Such innocence! But, now you stretch and yawn
And rise, you turn away from me toward
The somewhere-else that is to be endured.
The world is all before us. We shall meet
A messenger with news of our deceit
Where pale flowers shred and tangle on the thorn.

KIT WRIGHT

Poetry

When they say
That every day
Men die miserably without it:
I doubt it.

I have known several men and women
Replete with the stuff
Who died quite miserably
Enough.

And to hear of the human race's antennae!
Then I
Wonder what human race
They have in mind.
One of the poets I most admire
Is blind,
For instance. You wouldn't trust him
To lead you to the Gents:
Let alone through the future tense.

And unacknowledged legislators!
How's that for insane afflatus?
Not one I've met
Is the sort of bore
To wish to draft a law.

No, I like what vamped me
In my youth:
Tune, argument,
Colour, truth.